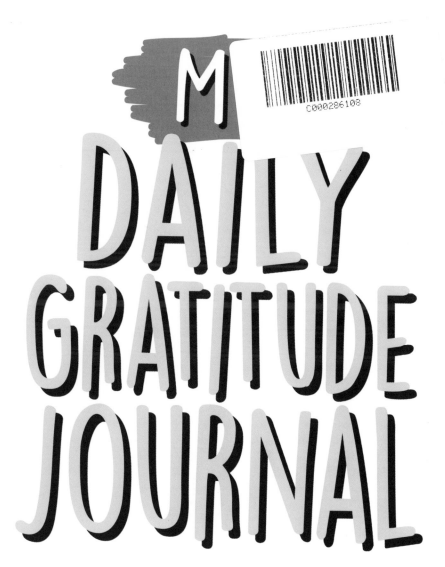

M

DAILY GRATITUDE JOURNAL

An Hachette UK Company
www.hachette.co.uk

Vie Books, an imprint of Summersdale Publishers Ltd
Part of Octopus Publishing Group Limited
Carmelite House
50 Victoria Embankment
LONDON
EC4Y 0DZ
UK

www.summersdale.com

Printed and bound in China

ISBN: 978-1-80007-770-6

Substantial discounts on bulk quantities of Summersdale books are available to corporations, professional associations and other organizations. For details contact general enquiries: telephone: +44 (0) 1243 771107 or email: enquiries@summersdale.com.

MY DAILY GRATITUDE JOURNAL

A fun, mood-boosting journal for kids

vie

INTRODUCTION

Welcome to *My Daily Gratitude Journal*! A place where you can record all the things that put a smile on your face, from the big things like spending time with friends or beating your personal best in sport, to the little things like a hilarious joke that you heard or cuddling a pet.

There are some amazing benefits to practising gratitude, from boosting self-esteem and lowering stress levels to feeling significantly happier.

Taking time to feel grateful is simple to do, and improves well-being and mood.

Let's get started!

HOW TO USE THIS JOURNAL

My Daily Gratitude Journal is for you, and you alone! There is a prompt for every day of the year, to help you fill it in and focus on your gratitude, whether it's first thing in the morning or last thing before bed – just choose between the sun and the moon symbols!

As you write in your journal, enjoy the calming benefits and happy vibes that gratitude brings to your life.

"PIGLET NOTICES THAT EVEN THOUGH HE HAD A VERY SMALL HEART, IT COULD HOLD A RATHER LARGE AMOUNT OF GRATITUDE."

Winnie-the-Pooh
A. A. Milne

What are you looking forward to this morning?

_____

_____

_____

_____

_____

What is a simple pleasure that you could enjoy today?

_____

_____

_____

_____

_____

_____

_____

_____

_____

_____

_____

_____

Describe your favourite moment of the day.

_____
_____
_____
_____
_____
_____
_____
_____
_____
_____
_____
_____
_____
_____

Who made you smile today?

Write something about your body for which you are grateful.

_____
_____
_____
_____
_____

_____
_____
_____
_____
_____

What act of kindness did you witness today?

Look out the window. What is something you are grateful for outside?

_____

_____

_____

_____

_____

Look around the room and list three things you love and are grateful for.

_____

_____

_____

_____

_____

_____

_____

_____

_____

_____

_____

_____

_____

_____

List three things you felt grateful for today.

Scroll through the photos on your phone or in a photo album and select a photo of a happy memory. Write down the memory here.

What did you feel proud about today?

Write about a time when you were brave.

"THIS IS A WONDERFUL DAY. I HAVE NEVER SEEN THIS ONE BEFORE."

Maya Angelou

Which person are you looking forward to seeing today?

_____

_____

_____

_____

_____

What possession makes your life easier?

_____

_____

_____

_____

_____

_____

_____

_____

_____

_____

_____

_____

Did you do anything today that made someone else happy?

What three words best describe your mood today?

_____

_____

_____

_____

_____

_____

_____

_____

_____

_____

_____

_____

_____

_____

_____

_____

_____

_____

_____

_____

_____

_____

_____

Have you seen anything that makes you happy today?

_____

_____

_____

_____

_____

_____

Write about one of the best experiences of your life.

How might you be able to help a friend today?

_____
_____
_____
_____
_____
_____

_____
_____
_____
_____
_____
_____

What made you grateful about nature today?

How are you feeling right now? Tick any that apply or add some of your own!

- [ ] STRESSED
- [ ] CONFIDENT
- [ ] HAPPY
- [ ] RELAXED
- [ ] OVERWHELMED
- [ ] ANGRY
- [ ] CREATIVE
- [ ] ANXIOUS
- [ ] LOVING
- [ ] HOPEFUL
- [ ] INSECURE
- [ ] MEH!
- [ ] SAD
- [ ] BALANCED
- [ ] _____
- [ ] _____

What's something you are grateful to have today that you didn't have a year ago?

_____

_____

_____

_____

_____

_____

_____

_____

_____

_____

Who makes you feel safe?

_____

Write down your favourite books here and why you like them.

Think of three things you are looking forward to today.

_____

_____

_____

_____

_____

_____

_____

_____

_____

_____

_____

Who's your favourite music artist at the moment?

_____

_____

Which friend are you feeling grateful for today?

Who makes you
laugh the most,
and why?

_____

_____

_____

_____

_____

_____

_____

_____

_____

_____

_____

_____

_____

_____

What is your
favourite piece of
clothing, and why?

_____

_____

_____

_____

_____

_____

_____

_____

_____

_____

_____

_____

_____

Which traditions
are you
grateful for?

Which aspect of your personality are you most grateful for?

_____

_____

_____

_____

_____

_____

How have you recently cared for your mental well-being?

_____

_____

_____

_____

_____

_____

_____

_____

_____

_____

_____

_____

_____

_____

Write down a mistake that turned out great!

"WHO DOES NOT THANK FOR LITTLE WILL NOT THANK FOR MUCH."

Estonian proverb

_____

_____

_____

_____

_____

_____

_____

_____

_____

_____

_____

_____

_____

What one thing would you like to accomplish today?

_____

_____

_____

_____

_____

_____

_____

_____

_____

_____

Which family member or friend are you most grateful for today, and why?

What did/do you love most about your father or grandfather?

Which skill are you looking forward to using today?

_____

_____

_____

_____

_____

What do you think will be the highlight of your day today?

_____

_____

_____

_____

_____

_____

_____

_____

_____

_____

_____

_____

What have you eaten today that has made you feel truly grateful?

Where is your favourite place to go to enjoy nature?

_____

_____

_____

_____

_____

Buy or cook a meal today that makes you feel grateful. What will you have?

_____

_____

_____

_____

_____

_____

_____

_____

_____

_____

_____

_____

What failure are you most grateful for now?

Write about a
time when you
felt lucky.

_____

_____

_____

_____

_____

_____

_____

_____

_____

_____

_____

What activity do
you enjoy doing most
with others?

How are you feeling right now?
Tick any that apply or add
some of your own!

- [ ] STRESSED
- [ ] CONFIDENT
- [ ] HAPPY
- [ ] RELAXED
- [ ] OVERWHELMED
- [ ] ANGRY
- [ ] CREATIVE
- [ ] ANXIOUS
- [ ] LOVING
- [ ] HOPEFUL
- [ ] INSECURE
- [ ] MEH!
- [ ] SAD
- [ ] BALANCED
- [ ] _____
- [ ] _____

What activity brings you the most joy?

_____

_____

_____

_____

_____

_____

Listen to one of your favourite songs. What do you love about it?

_____

_____

_____

_____

_____

_____

_____

_____

_____

_____

_____

_____

_____

_____

_____

_____

_____

What have you bought recently that you are grateful to own?

_____

_____

_____

_____

_____

Write about a time when you went out
of your way to help someone.

_____

_____

_____

_____

_____

_____

_____

_____

_____

_____

_____

_____

_____

What piece of
furniture are you
most grateful for?

Write down one good
thing that happened
to you today.

What do you love most about where you live?

_____

_____

_____

_____

_____

_____

_____

_____

_____

_____

_____

_____

What about your upbringing are you most grateful for this evening?

_____

_____

_____

_____

Overall, are you happy with the way your day turned out?

Write something about your body that you're grateful for.

_____
_____
_____
_____
_____
_____
_____
_____
_____
_____
_____
_____
_____
_____

Who has made you smile in the last few days?

_____
_____
_____
_____
_____

_____
_____
_____
_____
_____
_____

Did you have a nice surprise today? Write about it here.

It's time to take
a break. Have
some fun doodling
on these pages.

What is your favourite habit and why is it an important part of your daily routine?

_____

_____

_____

_____

_____

_____

_____

_____

_____

_____

_____

_____

_____

Write about something that made you smile today.

Describe a time when you felt truly at peace.

"The more you are in a state of gratitude, the more you will attract things to be grateful for."

Walt Disney

_____
_____
_____
_____
_____
_____
_____
_____
_____
_____
_____
_____
_____
_____
_____
_____

What was the highlight of your day?

What do you love most about your friends?

_____
_____
_____
_____
_____
_____

What did you feel proud of today?

_____
_____
_____
_____
_____
_____

What is your favourite part of your morning routine?

_____

_____

_____

_____

_____

_____

What one thing are you grateful for in your community?

_____

_____

_____

_____

_____

_____

_____

_____

_____

_____

_____

_____

Which one of your skills are you most grateful for this evening?

Name one thing about the weather you are grateful for today.

_____

_____

_____

_____

_____

_____

Have you felt lucky today?

_____

_____

_____

_____

_____

_____

How are you feeling right now?
Tick any that apply or add
some of your own!

- [ ] STRESSED
- [ ] CONFIDENT
- [ ] HAPPY
- [ ] RELAXED
- [ ] OVERWHELMED
- [ ] ANGRY
- [ ] CREATIVE
- [ ] ANXIOUS
- [ ] LOVING
- [ ] HOPEFUL
- [ ] INSECURE
- [ ] MEH!
- [ ] SAD
- [ ] BALANCED
- [ ] _____
- [ ] _____

Write about the last time you put off a task
that wasn't as bad as you thought it would be.

_____

_____

_____

_____

_____

_____

_____

_____

_____

_____

_____

_____

_____

What made you laugh
out loud today?

What one thing
have you learned in
the past few days that
you are grateful
to know?

What song are
you most grateful
for at the moment?

_____

_____

_____

_____

_____

_____

Which one of your
talents are you most
grateful for today?

_____

_____

_____

_____

_____

_____

_____

_____

_____

_____

_____

_____

_____

_____

_____

_____

_____

_____

_____

_____

_____

What is your favourite
part of your
evening routine?

What creature (animal or human) makes you happy this morning?

_____

_____

_____

_____

_____

_____

_____

_____

_____

_____

_____

_____

Which film do you feel the most gratitude for this evening?

_____

_____

_____

_____

_____

_____

What recent problem have you managed to overcome?

Is there anything you don't like about yourself? If so, can you think of one good thing about it?

_____

_____

_____

_____

Who is the person you would most like to connect with today?

_____

_____

_____

_____

_____

_____

_____

_____

_____

_____

_____

Think about someone who makes your life better.

What is your favourite word at the moment?

_____

_____

_____

_____

_____

_____

_____

_____

_____

_____

_____

Think of two skills you have that most people don't possess.

How are you feeling right now? Tick any that apply or add some of your own!

- [ ] STRESSED
- [ ] CONFIDENT
- [ ] HAPPY
- [ ] RELAXED
- [ ] OVERWHELMED
- [ ] ANGRY
- [ ] CREATIVE
- [ ] ANXIOUS
- [ ] LOVING
- [ ] HOPEFUL
- [ ] INSECURE
- [ ] MEH!
- [ ] SAD
- [ ] BALANCED
- [ ] _____
- [ ] _____

Can you think of the last time someone helped you with a problem?

_____
_____
_____
_____
_____
_____
_____

_____
_____
_____
_____
_____
_____

What has been your favourite holiday?

_____
_____
_____
_____
_____
_____

Write about someone who has made your life better.

How is your life
more positive today
than it was a year ago?

_____

_____

_____

_____

_____

_____

_____

_____

_____

_____

_____

_____

_____

_____

Think of a way
you can pamper yourself
today or this evening.

_____

_____

_____

_____

_____

_____

_____

_____

_____

_____

_____

When was the last
time you had a
real belly LAUGH?

What is the weather like today? Think of one positive thing to say about it.

_____

_____

_____

_____

_____

_____

What are you most grateful for this morning?

_____

_____

_____

_____

_____

_____

_____

_____

_____

_____

_____

_____

_____

Write down five simple things that make your life better that perhaps you take for granted, such as electricity, hot water and food.

"WHEN I PRAY, I ALWAYS THANK MOTHER NATURE FOR ALL THE BEAUTY IN THE WORLD. IT'S ABOUT HAVING AN ATTITUDE OF GRATITUDE."

Miranda Kerr

What kind things will you do for yourself today?

_____

_____

_____

_____

_____

_____

Write down something great that you have done that has made a big difference to someone.

Write about when a friend did something nice for you recently.

Think of the
last "perfect day"
you had.

_____

_____

_____

_____

_____

When was the
last time you woke up
feeling fully refreshed?

_____

_____

_____

_____

_____

_____

_____

_____

_____

_____

_____

_____

_____

What is one lesson you have learned
from a difficult situation?

Describe what you are most looking forward to at the end of today.

_____
_____
_____
_____
_____
_____

_____
_____
_____
_____
_____
_____

What's your favourite thing about school?

How are you feeling right now? Tick any that apply or add some of your own!

- [ ] STRESSED
- [ ] CONFIDENT
- [ ] HAPPY
- [ ] RELAXED
- [ ] OVERWHELMED
- [ ] ANGRY
- [ ] CREATIVE
- [ ] ANXIOUS
- [ ] LOVING
- [ ] HOPEFUL
- [ ] INSECURE
- [ ] MEH!
- [ ] SAD
- [ ] BALANCED
- [ ] _____
- [ ] _____

Describe the last time you worried about a task that was nowhere near as difficult as you first imagined.

_____
_____
_____
_____
_____
_____

_____
_____
_____
_____
_____

Who do you find the easiest to talk to at the moment?

_____
_____
_____
_____
_____

Who has forgiven you for a mistake you have made in the past?

When was the
last time you felt
courageous?

_____

_____

_____

_____

_____

_____

What's your
favourite breakfast
to start the day with?

_____

_____

_____

_____

_____

_____

_____

_____

_____

_____

_____

_____

_____

List the things you love most
about your bedroom.

What do you like best about the morning?

_____

_____

_____

_____

_____

_____

Describe a recent time when you truly felt at peace.

_____

_____

_____

_____

_____

How are you feeling right now? Tick any that apply or add some of your own!

- [ ] STRESSED
- [ ] CONFIDENT
- [ ] HAPPY
- [ ] RELAXED
- [ ] OVERWHELMED
- [ ] ANGRY
- [ ] CREATIVE
- [ ] ANXIOUS
- [ ] LOVING
- [ ] HOPEFUL
- [ ] INSECURE
- [ ] MEH!
- [ ] SAD
- [ ] BALANCED
- [ ] _____
- [ ] _____

What was the
last thank-you
note you wrote?

_____

_____

_____

_____

_____

_____

Can you think of
the last time
someone helped you
with a problem?

_____

_____

_____

_____

_____

_____

_____

_____

_____

_____

_____

_____

_____

_____

_____

_____

_____

_____

_____

_____

_____

_____

_____

_____

What is a
favourite quote
that you have come
across recently?

Think of one positive thing about this season.

_____

_____

_____

_____

_____

_____

_____

_____

_____

_____

_____

What makes you feel happy in the evening?

_____

_____

_____

_____

_____

_____

What is a drink you like best in the evening?

What makes you beautiful?

_____

_____

_____

_____

_____

_____

_____

Think of an experience that was difficult, but made you a stronger person.

_____

_____

_____

_____

_____

How are you feeling right now? Tick any that apply or add some of your own!

- [ ] STRESSED
- [ ] CONFIDENT
- [ ] HAPPY
- [ ] RELAXED
- [ ] OVERWHELMED
- [ ] ANGRY
- [ ] CREATIVE
- [ ] ANXIOUS
- [ ] LOVING
- [ ] HOPEFUL
- [ ] INSECURE
- [ ] MEH!
- [ ] SAD
- [ ] BALANCED
- [ ] _____
- [ ] _____

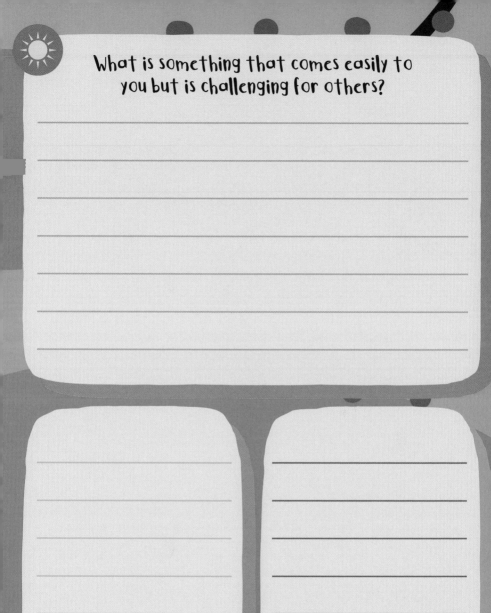

What is something that comes easily to you but is challenging for others?

_____
_____
_____
_____
_____
_____
_____

_____
_____
_____
_____
_____

Describe your favourite outfit and why it makes you feel great.

_____
_____
_____
_____
_____
_____

What activity do you enjoy most when you are alone?

How have you recently cared for
your physical well-being?

_____

_____

_____

_____

_____

_____

_____

_____

_____

Think about a
challenging person in
your life and write one
quality in them that
you appreciate.

What was the best
thing about being
a little child?

What app that you often use adds value to your life?

_____

_____

_____

_____

_____

_____

_____

_____

_____

_____

_____

_____

_____

_____

What is your favourite emotion to feel?

_____

_____

_____

_____

_____

What do you care about most today?

What is your
dream goal at
the moment?

_____

_____

_____

_____

_____

_____

What is something
that you have
recently fixed?

What is your
favourite game
to play?

Write about your favourite holiday.

_____

_____

_____

_____

_____

Which birthday has been the best so far?

_____

_____

_____

_____

_____

_____

_____

_____

_____

_____

_____

_____

_____

What worries do you have at the moment? How can you turn them to your advantage?

It's time to take a break. Have some fun doodling on these pages.

What is your favourite animal to observe in nature?

_____

_____

_____

_____

_____

Think about five things that you hope will happen in the coming year.

_____

_____

_____

_____

_____

_____

_____

_____

_____

_____

_____

_____

_____

_____

_____

_____

_____

What was the funniest joke you have heard recently?

_____

_____

_____

_____

_____

Think of something you could say to a friend to cheer them up if they are having a bad day.

_____
_____
_____
_____
_____
_____
_____

_____
_____
_____
_____
_____
_____

What is your favourite "me-time" activity?

_____
_____
_____
_____
_____
_____

What language would you most like to learn to speak?

What is your favourite sound?

_____

_____

_____

_____

_____

_____

_____

_____

_____

Picture your dream apartment. What would it look like? Where would it be?

_____

_____

_____

_____

_____

Who is your role model and why?

"ENOUGH IS A FEAST.

Buddhist proverb

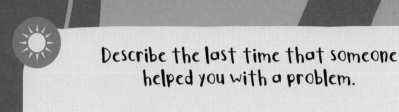

Describe the last time that someone helped you with a problem.

_____

_____

_____

_____

_____

_____

_____

_____

_____

_____

_____

_____

Is there a teacher you don't like? Think of two good things about them.

_____

_____

_____

_____

_____

_____

What is your favourite colour and how does it make you feel?

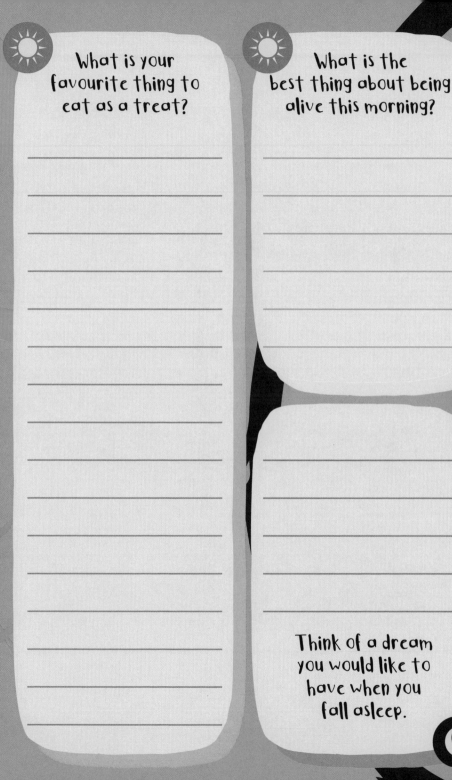

What is your favourite thing to eat as a treat?

What is the best thing about being alive this morning?

Think of a dream you would like to have when you fall asleep.

What cheers you up if you're feeling down?

_____
_____
_____
_____
_____

What is your favourite sense: sight, touch, hearing, smell or taste?

_____
_____
_____
_____
_____

_____
_____
_____
_____
_____
_____
_____

What freedoms are you most grateful for this evening?

What is your favourite flower today?

_____

_____

_____

_____

_____

_____

_____

How are you feeling right now? Tick any that apply or add some of your own!

- [ ] STRESSED
- [ ] CONFIDENT
- [ ] HAPPY
- [ ] RELAXED
- [ ] OVERWHELMED
- [ ] ANGRY
- [ ] CREATIVE
- [ ] ANXIOUS
- [ ] LOVING
- [ ] HOPEFUL
- [ ] INSECURE
- [ ] MEH!
- [ ] SAD
- [ ] BALANCED
- [ ] _____
- [ ] _____

What is something you've learned this week that has benefitted you?

What is your favourite TV show at the moment?

What did/do you love most about your mother/grandmother?

Who is the one friend you can always rely on?

Have you had a small win in the past couple of days?

_____

_____

_____

_____

_____

_____

What are you most looking forward to next month?

_____

_____

_____

_____

_____

_____

_____

_____

_____

_____

_____

What hobbies or activities would you miss if you could no longer do them?

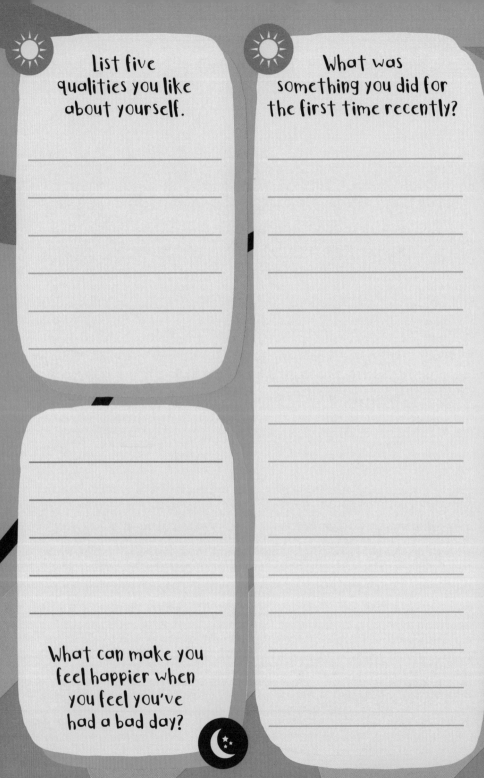

List five qualities you like about yourself.

_____

_____

_____

_____

_____

_____

What was something you did for the first time recently?

_____

_____

_____

_____

_____

_____

_____

_____

_____

_____

_____

_____

_____

_____

_____

_____

_____

_____

_____

_____

_____

_____

What can make you feel happier when you feel you've had a bad day?

What is the hardest thing you've ever had to do which led to something positive in your life?

_____
_____
_____
_____
_____
_____
_____

_____
_____
_____
_____
_____
_____

Who made you smile in the last couple of days and why?

_____
_____
_____
_____
_____
_____

Can you think of a way to show your gratitude?

What is a great recipe that you've prepared that others loved?

_____
_____
_____
_____
_____
_____

What is your favourite way to enjoy nature and the outdoors?

_____
_____
_____
_____
_____
_____

_____
_____
_____
_____
_____
_____
_____

Write about someone you've never met but who has helped your life in some way.

"BE THANKFUL FOR WHAT YOU HAVE; YOU'LL END UP HAVING MORE. IF YOU CONCENTRATE ON WHAT YOU DON'T HAVE, YOU WILL NEVER, EVER HAVE ENOUGH."

Oprah Winfrey

What gift have you enjoyed receiving in the last year?

_____
_____
_____
_____
_____
_____

What opportunities are you most grateful for today?

_____
_____
_____
_____
_____
_____
_____
_____
_____
_____
_____
_____
_____
_____
_____
_____

What is your favourite film at the moment?

_____
_____
_____
_____
_____

Think of a small, everyday activity that you enjoy with another person in your life.

_____

_____

_____

_____

_____

_____

_____

_____

_____

_____

_____

Can you think of an obstacle you have faced and how you overcame it?

_____

_____

_____

_____

_____

_____

_____

Write about someone who makes your life better.

It's time to take
a break. Have
some fun doodling
on these pages.

How could you show gratitude for the amazing people in your life?

_____
_____
_____
_____
_____
_____
_____

_____
_____
_____
_____
_____
_____

Describe a weird family tradition that makes you happy.

_____
_____
_____
_____
_____
_____

What's your favourite way to relax?

What bit of information are you glad to know?

_____

_____

_____

_____

_____

_____

_____

_____

_____

_____

_____

_____

_____

Describe a piece of positive news you recently heard.

_____

_____

_____

_____

_____

_____

_____

_____

_____

_____

_____

_____

Describe a funny YouTube video that you've recently watched.

_____
_____
_____
_____
_____
_____
_____
_____
_____
_____
_____
_____
_____
_____

Write about a time when you felt courageous.

What is your favourite pet?

_____
_____
_____
_____
_____
_____
_____

_____
_____
_____
_____
_____
_____

Where is your happy place?

What is something you are looking forward to at the moment?

What is a simple pleasure that you could enjoy today?

Describe an experience that was difficult but ultimately made you stronger.

What about your childhood makes you feel grateful?

_____

_____

_____

_____

_____

Look out the window. What's something you are grateful for outside?

_____

_____

_____

_____

_____

_____

_____

_____

_____

_____

_____

Think of your oldest friend and what they bring to your life.

What possession makes your life easier?

_____

_____

_____

_____

_____

_____

_____

Name something beautiful you saw today.

_____

_____

_____

_____

_____

How are you feeling right now? Tick any that apply or add some of your own!

- [ ] STRESSED
- [ ] CONFIDENT
- [ ] HAPPY
- [ ] RELAXED
- [ ] OVERWHELMED
- [ ] ANGRY
- [ ] CREATIVE
- [ ] ANXIOUS
- [ ] LOVING
- [ ] HOPEFUL
- [ ] INSECURE
- [ ] MEH!
- [ ] SAD
- [ ] BALANCED
- [ ] _____
- [ ] _____

What person are you looking forward to seeing today?

_____
_____
_____
_____
_____
_____

What is the best bit of your day?

_____
_____
_____
_____
_____
_____
_____
_____
_____
_____
_____
_____
_____
_____

_____
_____
_____
_____
_____
_____

What memory are you grateful for today?

What are the three best things to have happened to you so far this year?

_____

_____

_____

_____

_____

_____

_____

_____

_____

_____

_____

_____

What small thing happened today that you are grateful for?

Name a basic need which has been met today.

Look around the room and list three
things that you're grateful for.

_____

_____

_____

_____

_____

_____

_____

_____

_____

_____

_____

_____

What is the best
thing about being
the age you are?

Describe your
favourite moment
of the day.

What was the last thank-you note you received?

_____

_____

_____

_____

_____

_____

_____

_____

_____

_____

_____

_____

What is something you are grateful to have today that you didn't have a year ago?

_____

_____

_____

_____

_____

_____

_____

_____

_____

_____

_____

Describe your favourite person of the day.

It's time to take a break. Have some fun doodling on these pages.

How might you
be able to help
others today?

_____

_____

_____

_____

_____

What act of
kindness did you
witness today?

_____

_____

_____

_____

_____

_____

_____

_____

_____

_____

_____

_____

Write down three things
you feel grateful
for today.

_____

_____

_____

_____

_____

Which of your values are you most grateful for?

_____

_____

_____

_____

_____

Write about something kind you have done for yourself today.

_____

_____

_____

_____

_____

_____

_____

_____

_____

_____

_____

_____

What did you feel proud of today?

"DON'T TRY SO HARD TO FIT IN, AND CERTAINLY DON'T TRY TO BE DIFFERENT: JUST TRY TO BE YOU."

Zendaya

Think about a time when you went out of your way to help someone.

_____

_____

_____

_____

_____

_____

_____

_____

_____

_____

Did you do anything today that made someone else happy?

What has been your favourite weekend?

What nice things have you done for yourself lately?

_____

_____

_____

_____

_____

_____

What meal would you cook today to show how grateful you are for your loved ones?

_____

_____

_____

_____

_____

How are you feeling right now? Tick any that apply or add some of your own!

- [ ] STRESSED
- [ ] CONFIDENT
- [ ] HAPPY
- [ ] RELAXED
- [ ] OVERWHELMED
- [ ] ANGRY
- [ ] CREATIVE
- [ ] ANXIOUS
- [ ] LOVING
- [ ] HOPEFUL
- [ ] INSECURE
- [ ] MEH!
- [ ] SAD
- [ ] BALANCED
- [ ] _____
- [ ] _____

Reflect on some of the best experiences of your life.

_____

_____

_____

_____

_____

_____

_____

_____

_____

_____

_____

_____

_____

_____

Have you seen anything that makes you happy today?

_____

_____

_____

_____

_____

_____

Who makes you feel safe?

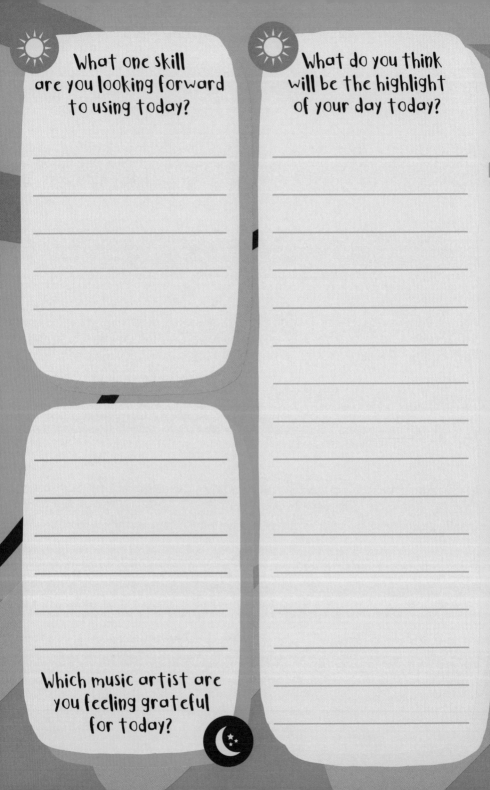

What one skill are you looking forward to using today?

What do you think will be the highlight of your day today?

Which music artist are you feeling grateful for today?

Find something that makes you happy in nature today.

_____
_____
_____
_____
_____
_____
_____

_____
_____
_____
_____
_____
_____

Which books make you feel good?

_____
_____
_____
_____
_____
_____

Which friend are you feeling grateful towards today?

What one thing would you like to accomplish today?

_____

_____

_____

_____

_____

Think about a time when you felt lucky.

_____

_____

_____

_____

_____

_____

_____

_____

_____

_____

_____

What special days and festivals do you most look forward to?

Which outfit makes you feel your best?

_____

_____

_____

_____

_____

_____

What mistake are you grateful for this week?

_____

_____

_____

_____

_____

How are you feeling right now? Tick any that apply or add some of your own!

- [ ] STRESSED
- [ ] CONFIDENT
- [ ] HAPPY
- [ ] RELAXED
- [ ] OVERWHELMED
- [ ] ANGRY
- [ ] CREATIVE
- [ ] ANXIOUS
- [ ] LOVING
- [ ] HOPEFUL
- [ ] INSECURE
- [ ] MEH!
- [ ] SAD
- [ ] BALANCED
- [ ] _____
- [ ] _____

What makes you feel most grateful about the area in which you live?

_____

_____

_____

_____

_____

_____

_____

_____

_____

_____

_____

_____

What new thing have you learnt today?

_____

_____

_____

_____

_____

What do you love most about your brother/sister?

What activity brings you the most joy?

_____

_____

_____

_____

_____

_____

_____

_____

_____

_____

_____

_____

_____

_____

_____

Listen to one of your favourite songs from childhood. Why does it make you feel good?

_____

_____

_____

_____

_____

_____

_____

_____

_____

_____

_____

_____

_____

What skills or talents are you most proud of?

Write down
three things that fill
you with joy today.

_____

_____

_____

_____

_____

_____

Who has
made you smile in
the last few days?

_____

_____

_____

_____

_____

_____

_____

_____

_____

_____

_____

_____

_____

Has anything happened to you that seemed bad luck
at the time that was ultimately good for you?

"STRIVE TO FIND THINGS TO BE THANKFUL FOR, AND JUST LOOK FOR THE GOOD IN WHO YOU ARE."

Bethany Hamilton

_____
_____
_____
_____
_____
_____
_____
_____
_____
_____
_____
_____
_____
_____

When you look around, can you see an object that makes you feel safe and cared for?

_____
_____
_____
_____

What activity do you enjoy most when with others?

What have you bought recently that you are grateful to own?

Think about why your friends like you.

_____

_____

_____

_____

_____

Why are you grateful for your eyes?

_____

_____

_____

_____

_____

_____

_____

_____

_____

_____

_____

_____

What object are you most grateful for at the moment?

It's time to take a break. Have some fun doodling on these pages.

What is your
favourite part of your
morning routine?

_____
_____
_____
_____
_____
_____

What one thing
are you grateful for
in your country?

_____
_____
_____
_____
_____
_____
_____
_____
_____
_____
_____
_____
_____
_____
_____

_____
_____
_____
_____
_____
_____

Write down one good
thing that happened
to you today.

Which one of your talents are you most grateful for today?

_____

_____

_____

_____

_____

_____

_____

_____

_____

_____

_____

_____

_____

Who are you most grateful for in your life?

_____

_____

_____

_____

_____

Overall, are you happy with the way your day turned out?

Think of the last time you put off a task
that wasn't as bad as you thought it would be.

_____

_____

_____

_____

_____

_____

_____

_____

_____

_____

_____

_____

Did you have a nice
surprise today?

Think about
something that made
you smile today.

What song are you most grateful for at the moment?

_____
_____
_____
_____
_____
_____
_____
_____
_____
_____
_____
_____
_____
_____

What's your favourite thing about mornings?

_____
_____
_____
_____
_____
_____

What do you love most about being you?

_____
_____
_____
_____
_____

What creature (animal or human) makes you happy this morning?

_____
_____
_____
_____
_____
_____

_____
_____
_____
_____
_____
_____

Have you felt lucky today?

How are you feeling right now? Tick any that apply or add some of your own!

- [ ] STRESSED
- [ ] CONFIDENT
- [ ] HAPPY
- [ ] RELAXED
- [ ] OVERWHELMED
- [ ] ANGRY
- [ ] CREATIVE
- [ ] ANXIOUS
- [ ] LOVING
- [ ] HOPEFUL
- [ ] INSECURE
- [ ] MEH!
- [ ] SAD
- [ ] BALANCED
- [ ] _____
- [ ] _____

What is your favourite habit and why is it an important part of your daily routine?

_____

_____

_____

_____

_____

_____

_____

_____

_____

_____

_____

_____

What type of food brought you joy today?

_____

_____

_____

_____

_____

What made you happy about nature today?

How is your life
more positive today
than it was a year ago?

What made
you laugh out
loud today?

What is your
favourite part of your
evening routine?

Who is the person
you would most like to
connect with today?

_____

_____

_____

_____

_____

Think of a way
you can pamper yourself
today or this evening.

_____

_____

_____

_____

_____

_____

_____

_____

_____

_____

_____

_____

Write about something new that
brightened your day.

What book have you read recently that inspired you?

_____

_____

_____

_____

_____

What is your favourite season?

_____

_____

_____

_____

_____

_____

_____

_____

_____

_____

_____

_____

_____

What movie are you the most grateful for at the moment?

Write down something great about yourself here.

_____

_____

_____

_____

_____

_____

_____

_____

_____

What recent problem have you managed to overcome?

How are you feeling right now? Tick any that apply or add some of your own!

- [ ] STRESSED
- [ ] CONFIDENT
- [ ] HAPPY
- [ ] RELAXED
- [ ] OVERWHELMED
- [ ] ANGRY
- [ ] CREATIVE
- [ ] ANXIOUS
- [ ] LOVING
- [ ] HOPEFUL
- [ ] INSECURE
- [ ] MEH!
- [ ] SAD
- [ ] BALANCED
- [ ] _____
- [ ] _____

What is your biggest dream at the moment?

_____

_____

_____

_____

_____

_____

_____

_____

_____

_____

_____

_____

Think about someone who makes your life better.

How are you feeling right now? Tick any that apply or add some of your own!

- [ ] STRESSED
- [ ] CONFIDENT
- [ ] HAPPY
- [ ] RELAXED
- [ ] OVERWHELMED
- [ ] ANGRY
- [ ] CREATIVE
- [ ] ANXIOUS
- [ ] LOVING
- [ ] HOPEFUL
- [ ] INSECURE
- [ ] MEH!
- [ ] SAD
- [ ] BALANCED
- [ ] _____
- [ ] _____

What is your favourite song at the moment?

_____

_____

_____

_____

_____

_____

_____

_____

_____

_____

Think of two skills you have that most people don't possess.

Think of your oldest friend and what they bring to your life.

Think of the last "perfect day" you had.

_____
_____
_____
_____
_____
_____

When was the last time you woke up feeling fully refreshed?

_____
_____
_____
_____
_____
_____
_____
_____
_____
_____
_____
_____
_____
_____

_____
_____
_____
_____
_____
_____

Write about someone who has made your life better.

Describe the last time you worried about
a task that was nowhere near as
difficult as you first imagined.

_____

_____

_____

_____

_____

_____

_____

_____

_____

_____

_____

_____

What's the best
piece of advice you
received today?

What is a drink
that you like best
in the evening?

"I CAN NO OTHER ANSWER MAKE, BUT, THANKS, AND THANKS, AND EVER THANKS."

William Shakespeare

Describe what you are most looking forward to at the end of today.

_____

_____

_____

_____

_____

_____

_____

_____

_____

_____

_____

_____

What's your favourite subject at school at the moment?

_____

_____

_____

_____

_____

_____

Name something beautiful you saw today.

Think of one positive thing about this season.

_____

_____

_____

_____

_____

_____

_____

_____

_____

_____

_____

_____

_____

_____

_____

Write about a recent time when a friend did something nice for you.

What's the nicest compliment you received today?

What do you like best about the morning?

_____

_____

_____

_____

_____

_____

_____

_____

_____

_____

_____

_____

_____

_____

Who will you look to for inspiration today?

_____

_____

_____

_____

_____

_____

_____

_____

_____

_____

_____

_____

What is one lesson we can learn from someone who is unkind?

What is your favourite season?

_____

_____

_____

_____

_____

_____

_____

What makes you beautiful?

_____

_____

_____

_____

_____

_____

_____

_____

_____

_____

_____

_____

_____

_____

_____

What do you love most about your life today?

What is the nicest thing you can say to yourself this morning?

_____

_____

_____

_____

_____

_____

Who has forgiven you for a mistake you have made in the past?

_____

_____

_____

_____

_____

How are you feeling right now? Tick any that apply or add some of your own!

- [ ] STRESSED
- [ ] CONFIDENT
- [ ] HAPPY
- [ ] RELAXED
- [ ] OVERWHELMED
- [ ] ANGRY
- [ ] CREATIVE
- [ ] ANXIOUS
- [ ] LOVING
- [ ] HOPEFUL
- [ ] INSECURE
- [ ] MEH!
- [ ] SAD
- [ ] BALANCED
- [ ] _____
- [ ] _____

What app that you often use adds value to your life?

_____

_____

_____

_____

_____

Describe a recent time when you felt peaceful.

What do you like best about the evening?

How have you recently cared for your physical well-being?

_____

_____

_____

_____

_____

What is something that comes easily to you but is challenging for others?

_____

_____

_____

_____

_____

_____

_____

_____

_____

_____

_____

_____

What is something positive you can learn from one of your negative qualities?

What is your favourite emotion to feel?

_____

_____

_____

_____

_____

_____

How are you feeling right now? Tick any that apply or add some of your own!

- [ ] STRESSED
- [ ] CONFIDENT
- [ ] HAPPY
- [ ] RELAXED
- [ ] OVERWHELMED
- [ ] ANGRY
- [ ] CREATIVE
- [ ] ANXIOUS
- [ ] LOVING
- [ ] HOPEFUL
- [ ] INSECURE
- [ ] MEH!
- [ ] SAD
- [ ] BALANCED
- [ ] _____
- [ ] _____

_____

_____

_____

_____

What is a favourite quote that you have come across recently?

What body part are you most grateful for this morning?

_____

_____

_____

_____

_____

_____

_____

_____

_____

_____

What is your favourite bedtime routine?

_____

_____

_____

_____

Think of an experience that was difficult, but made you a stronger person.

What would be your dream job?

_____

_____

_____

_____

_____

_____

_____

Which party has been the best so far?

_____

_____

_____

_____

_____

_____

_____

_____

_____

_____

_____

_____

_____

_____

_____

_____

_____

_____

Describe your favourite outfit and why it makes you feel great.

_____

_____

_____

_____

_____

Think of something you could say to a friend, to cheer them up if they are having a bad day.

_____

_____

_____

_____

_____

_____

_____

_____

_____

_____

_____

_____

What activity do you enjoy most when you are alone?

What is your dream holiday destination?

"NEVER LET SUCCESS GO TO YOUR HEAD. NEVER LET FAILURE GO TO YOUR HEART."

Beyoncé

What do you love to do when the sun is shining?

_____

_____

_____

_____

_____

_____

What was the funniest joke you have heard recently?

_____

_____

_____

_____

_____

_____

_____

_____

_____

_____

_____

_____

Think about a challenging person in your life and write one quality in them that you appreciate.

It's time to take a break. Have some fun doodling on these pages.

Describe the last time that someone
helped you with a problem.

_____

_____

_____

_____

_____

_____

_____

_____   _____

_____   _____

_____   _____

_____   _____

_____   _____

_____   _____

Why do you support the   What is something
charities that you   that you have
do or intend to?   recently fixed?

What is your favourite sound?

_____

_____

_____

_____

_____

_____

_____

_____

_____

_____

_____

_____

_____

_____

_____

What is your favourite flower today?

_____

_____

_____

_____

_____

_____

_____

_____

_____

_____

_____

_____

_____

What is your favourite game to play?

_____
_____
_____
_____
_____
_____
_____
_____
_____
_____
_____
_____
_____

Write down five things that you hope will happen in the next year.

What is your favourite thing to eat as a treat?

_____
_____
_____
_____
_____
_____

What is your favourite fun activity?

_____
_____
_____
_____
_____

What is the best
thing about being
alive this morning?

_____
_____
_____
_____
_____
_____

What cheers you
up if you feel you're
having an attack
of the "blues"?

_____
_____
_____
_____
_____
_____

_____
_____
_____
_____
_____
_____

What worries do you have at the moment?
How can you turn them to your advantage?

Describe your favourite sensation.

_____

_____

_____

_____

_____

Which of your physical features do you like best?

_____

_____

_____

_____

_____

_____

_____

_____

_____

_____

_____

Picture your dream job.
What are doing? Where will you be?

What is your
favourite TV show
at the moment?

_____

_____

_____

_____

_____

_____

_____

_____

_____

_____

What language would
you most like to
learn to speak?

How are you feeling right now?
Tick any that apply or add
some of your own!

- [ ] STRESSED
- [ ] CONFIDENT
- [ ] HAPPY
- [ ] RELAXED
- [ ] OVERWHELMED
- [ ] ANGRY
- [ ] CREATIVE
- [ ] ANXIOUS
- [ ] LOVING
- [ ] HOPEFUL
- [ ] INSECURE
- [ ] MEH!
- [ ] SAD
- [ ] BALANCED
- [ ] _____
- [ ] _____

List five
qualities you like
about yourself.

_____

_____

_____

_____

_____

_____

What are you
most looking forward
to next month?

_____

_____

_____

_____

_____

_____

_____

_____

_____

_____

_____

_____

_____

_____

_____

_____

_____

How does your
favourite colour
make you feel?

What is the hardest thing you've ever had to do which led to something positive in your life?

_____
_____
_____
_____
_____
_____
_____

_____
_____
_____
_____
_____
_____

Think of a person you would like to be friends with.

_____
_____
_____
_____
_____

Think of a dream you would like to have when you fall asleep.

"GRATITUDE LOOKS TO THE PAST AND LOVE TO THE PRESENT."

C. S. Lewis

What is your favourite way to enjoy nature and the outdoors?

_____

_____

_____

_____

_____

_____

_____

_____

_____

_____

**What freedoms are
you most grateful
for this evening?**

_____

_____

_____

_____

_____

_____

**What memory
are you grateful
for today?**

Think of a small, everyday thing that you enjoy with another person in your life.

_____
_____
_____
_____
_____
_____

_____
_____
_____
_____
_____

What can make you
feel happier when
you feel you've
had a bad day?

_____
_____
_____
_____
_____

What hobbies or
activities would you
miss if you could no
longer do them?

Have you had a
small win in the past
couple of days?

_____

_____

_____

_____

_____

_____

_____

_____

_____

_____

_____

_____

_____

What
opportunities are
you grateful for
this morning?

_____

_____

_____

_____

_____

_____

_____

_____

_____

_____

_____

_____

What do you love
most about your
best friend?

When was the last time you felt courageous?

_____
_____
_____
_____
_____
_____

What three ways do you like to express yourself creatively?

_____
_____
_____
_____

How are you feeling right now? Tick any that apply or add some of your own!

- [ ] STRESSED
- [ ] CONFIDENT
- [ ] HAPPY
- [ ] RELAXED
- [ ] OVERWHELMED
- [ ] ANGRY
- [ ] CREATIVE
- [ ] ANXIOUS
- [ ] LOVING
- [ ] HOPEFUL
- [ ] INSECURE
- [ ] MEH!
- [ ] SAD
- [ ] BALANCED
- [ ] _____
- [ ] _____

What is a great recipe that you've prepared that others loved?

_____
_____
_____
_____
_____
_____
_____

What is something you've learned this week that has benefitted you?

_____
_____
_____
_____

Who made you smile in the last couple of days and why?

_____
_____
_____
_____

☀

Describe a piece of positive news you recently heard.

_____

_____

_____

_____

_____

_____

_____

_____

_____

_____

_____

_____

_____

_____

_____

_____

_____

_____

_____

_____

_____

_____

_____

_____

_____

_____

_____

_____

Think of a way you can share your gratitude with others. 🌙

What is your favourite film at the moment? 🌙

What piece of information are you glad to know?

_____

_____

_____

_____

_____

What gift have you enjoyed receiving in the last year?

_____

_____

_____

_____

_____

_____

_____

_____

_____

_____

_____

_____

_____

Write about someone you've never met but who has helped your life in some way.

"GRATITUDE IS THE CLOSEST THING TO BEAUTY MANIFESTED AS AN EMOTION."

Mindy Kaling

What are you most looking forward to today?

_____

_____

_____

_____

_____

_____

What are your three favourite smells?

_____

_____

_____

_____

_____

_____

_____

_____

_____

_____

_____

_____

Can you think of an obstacle you have faced and how you overcame it?

What is the nicest
thing that someone has
said to you recently?

Which of your
physical features
do you like best?

Write about someone
who makes your
life better.

Think of three things you are looking forward to this morning.

_____

_____

_____

_____

_____

_____

_____

_____

_____

_____

Describe a weird family tradition that makes you happy.

What small act of kindness could you do for a friend tomorrow?

How could you show gratitude for the amazing people in your life?

_____

_____

_____

_____

_____

_____

_____

_____

_____

_____

_____

_____

Describe a funny YouTube video that you've recently watched.

_____

_____

_____

What small thing happened today that you're grateful for?